Practical Wisdom

Learning Life's Lessons from the Simple, But Profound Things We Hear Every Day

John Leonard Harris, Sr.

Lulu.com

All the best and much success!

John
aka
"Mr Encouragement"

CREDITS

IBSN: 978-1-387-47289-5

Although the author and publisher have made every effort to ensure that the information in this book was correct at press time, the author and publisher do not assume and hereby disclaim any liability to any party for any loss, damage, or disruption caused by errors or omissions, whether such errors or omissions result from negligence, accident, or any other cause.

The Holy Bible, New King James Version®. Copyright © 1982 by Thomas Nelson, Inc. All rights reserved.

The text of the New King James Version® (NKJV®) may be quoted or reprinted without prior written permission with the following qualifications:

(1) Up to and including 1,000 verses may be quoted in printed form as long as the verses quoted amount to less than 50% of a complete book of the Bible and make up less than 50% of the total work in which they are quoted; (2) all NKJV quotations must conform accurately to the NKJV text.

Any use of the NKJV text must include a proper acknowledgment as follows:
"Scripture taken from the New King James Version. Copyright © 1982 by Thomas Nelson, Inc. Used by permission. All rights reserved."

However, when quotations from the NKJV text are used in church bulletins, orders of service, Sunday School lessons, church newsletters and similar works in the course of religious instruction or services at a place of worship or other religious assembly, the following notice may be used at the end of each quotation: "NKJV."

For quotations requests not covered by the above guidelines, write to: Thomas Nelson Publishers. Attention: Bible Rights and Permissions, P. O. Box 141000, Nashville, TN 37214-1000.

For further information and guidelines, please go to:
http://www.thomasnelson.com/consumer/dept.asp?dept_id=190660&TopLevel_id=190000

WHAT'S INSIDE?

Dedications	p. 5
Acknowledgments	p. 6
Special Dedications	p. 7
Introduction	p. 8-9
Why This Book?	p. 10
Father Ralph Wright	p. 11
Maeola (Harris) Blanchard	p. 15
Frederick Douglass	p. 19
Rev. Dr. Martin Luther King, Jr.	p. 23
Proverbs 16:18	p. 27
Anonymous	p. 31
Dr. Myles Munroe	p. 35
Samuel Smiles	p. 39
Ralph Ellison	p. 43
E. Alan Jacobsen	p. 47
Adlai Stevenson	p. 51
John James Beckley	p. 55
Maeola (Harris) Blanchard	p. 59
William Blake	p. 63
Denzel Washington	p. 67
Chinese Proverb	p. 71
Thomas Edison	p. 75
Marcus Fabious Quintilianus	p. 79
Virgil (Stubby) Currence	p. 83
Rev. Dr. Martin Luther King, Jr.	p. 87
Maeola (Harris) Blanchard	p. 91
E. Alan Jacobsen	p. 95
Will Rogers	p. 99
Hilary Hinton "Zig" Ziglar	p. 103
Practical Wisdom from John	p. 107
Make Your Own "Practical Wisdom"	p. 115
About the Author	p. 120

DEDICATION

To my mother, Maeola (Harris) Blanchard. She is my hero! She is the wisest and hardest working person that I have ever known. She stressed the importance of faith, family, and education. Her sacrifice has helped me to be who I am today. Her example of love and faith has shown me the person of Jesus Christ in a real and tangible way. I am so grateful to her!

To my lovely wife, Charlene. No one has been as supportive and encouraging as my wife. No one believes in me more and would have taken the journey that we have taken together. I love Charlene so much and will be forever grateful to her for being the person who inspires me.

ACKNOWLEDGMENTS

To my **Lord and Savior Jesus Christ**, the one who died for my sins so that I might live in Him. I am so thankful for every day God wakes me up and helps me to live as a person with a genuine passion for life and clear sense of purpose.

To my children, **Preston, Shannon, JoAnna and John Jr.** I am so proud of each of you and consider it a privilege to be your father. Remember, **"Excellence is the Only Option!"** Also, to my grandsons, Eli, Legend and Owen, "papa loves you!"

My father, **Elder Eugene H. Harris, Jr.,** who was a strong, proud man. He believed in me and told me that I would preach one day, and he was right. My sisters **(Gwen, Regina, Chrystal, Lisa)** and brothers **(Chris, Tim),** whom I love. All my **nephews, nieces, cousins and in-laws** that make up the family I love so much.

To my teachers and friends from **Wellston, Missouri** who are among the greatest people that I have ever known. To the monks and my **St. Louis Priory** classmates. My **professors** and **fellow Mizzou alums**, who were a part of the craziest years of my life while attending the University of Missouri-Columbia.

And finally, to all of the staff and students that have impacted my life at **Dartmouth College,** and the **Universities of Nebraska** in **Omaha** and **Lincoln.**

SPECIAL DEDICATIONS

Special people to me who have passed on from this life, but not from my memory.

Senator JoAnn Maxey

Angela Marie Harris

Mr. and Mrs. Robert Adams

Keith Bernard Clair, Sr.

Warren ("Krazy Man") Koonce

Pastor Alan Jacobsen

Rev. Don Coleman

Nathan ("Nate the Skate") Johns

Steve Schneider

Jarvis Long

Gary Hassebrook

Obasi Onuoha

Charles H. Bowling

INTRODUCTION

Often, after many of my speaking engagements people would approach me and ask, **"Would you tell me again who said the quote or phrase that you used in your presentation?"** Well, after plus years, I finally figured out the best way to help people remember the things I have said and the people who said them.

This book allows me the opportunity to let you into my world, a world of words. I love words and the **"power of words"** to encourage and inspire others.

I remember my seventh-grade teacher, Mr. Riley making our class write the **eight parts of speech** on the blackboard daily. I remember one of my best friends, Kent and I playing **Hangman**; always trying to outdo one another with difficult words to win the game. We really worked hard at trying to beat one another.

When I founded my nonprofit organization, Encouragement Unlimited, Inc. in 2002, I knew that I would have countless opportunities to reach people with **"words of encouragement"** and **"messages of hope."** Over the years since our inception, I have used words and a 4 x 6 postcard to let over 15,000 people know the **"power of encouragement."**

As you read through the quotes and phrases that I have provided in this book, think about the ones that you have heard people say and some of the things that you have said yourself. If you really think about it, you have probably said things that can provide great lessons for other people.

If you don't get anything else from this book, know this. The words might inspire, but the key is what you do with it afterwards. You must take what you read and apply it to your life.

Lastly, God has given me with the privilege of encouraging others . . . that's what I do. I pray that the whole book blesses you, however, even if one of the quotes or phrases makes a difference for you . . . I have done my job!

My favorite quote is actually a scripture verse from Galatians 2:20 (NKJV)

"I have been crucified with Christ; it is no longer I who live, but Christ lives in me; and the life which I now live in the flesh I live by faith in the Son of God, who loved me and gave Himself for me."

WHY THIS BOOK?

Practical Wisdom is a book of the quotes that have meant so much to me over the course of my life. I have realized that there are times when the simplest thought or phrase can remind you of what is important, reduce the anxiety that you are feeling or spur you to action. That is what this book is all about.

It is my desire that as you read each bit of ***"practical wisdom"*** that I have shared here, that you find something that connects in each one. I have provided you with several pages to make your own notes. As you read these quotes, think about how they might best apply to you. Also, use your own notes as a reminder of the practical and simple lessons that you must apply in real life.

Do not make your journey through this book a one- time occurrence. Come back again and again. Reaffirm for yourself those fundamental and foundational truths that can truly help you to be your best every single day.

Some people need advice that challenges them to think differently about life. Some need that which calls to their soul. And still others need words, so simple and applicable for real life in real time. I call that **"Practical Wisdom!"**

"What does the world need and what gift has God given me to provide it?"

**Father Ralph Wright, O.S.B.
St. Louis Priory**

"During my own personal search for purpose in life there was no more important question than the words in this quote. After reading it, I knew that the world would need more encouragement and that I would be its provider."

YOUR REFLECTION

What is the first thing that came to your mind as you read the quote?

_____

_____

_____

_____

_____

YOUR REACTION

Is there a lesson in this quote for you?

_____

_____

_____

_____

_____

YOUR RESPONSE

What are three things that you can do to use this Practical Wisdom in your daily life?

- _____
  _____
  _____

- _____
  _____
  _____

- _____
  _____
  _____

"Everything you can say, isn't something you should say."

Maeola (Harris) Blanchard
My mother and my hero

"My mother becomes a great deal wiser the older I get. The wisdom of this quote suggests that "words have power" and it is important to think before you speak. Her words remind me to be careful with not only what I say, but how I say it."

YOUR REFLECTION

What is the first thing that came to your mind as you read the quote?

_____

_____

_____

_____

_____

YOUR REACTION

Is there a lesson in this quote for you?

_____

_____

_____

_____

_____

YOUR RESPONSE

What are three things that you can do to use this Practical Wisdom in your daily life?

- _____
  _____
  _____
  _____

- _____
  _____
  _____
  _____

- _____
  _____

> *"If there is no struggle, there is no progress."*
>
> *Frederick Douglass*
> *Statesman, Orator, Abolitionist*
> *1818 -1895*

"This quote from Frederick Douglass reminds me of what it often takes to advance in life. The progress that we want to see rarely occurs without overcoming some form of adversity. Over the course of my life I have found that faith, perseverance and resilience have been key aspects of any success that I have had."

YOUR REFLECTION

What is the first thing that came to your mind as you read the quote?

_____

_____

_____

_____

_____

YOUR REACTION

Is there a lesson in this quote for you?

_____

_____

_____

_____

_____

YOUR RESPONSE

What are three things that you can do to use this Practical Wisdom in your daily life?

- _____

  _____

  _____

  _____

- _____

  _____

  _____

  _____

- _____

"The ultimate measure of a man is not where he stands in moments of comfort and convenience, but where he stands at times of challenge and controversy."

*Rev. Dr. Martin Luther King, Jr.
Civil Rights Leader
1929 - 1968*

"Dr. King's quote reminds me that anyone can take the easy road. However, to make things happen you cannot sit back and watch others do all the heavy lifting. To be a difference maker you may have to get your hands dirty and put yourself on the line. You cannot always take the easy way out."

YOUR REFLECTION

What is the first thing that came to your mind as you read the quote?

_____
_____
_____
_____
_____

YOUR REACTION

Is there a lesson in this quote for you?

_____
_____
_____
_____
_____

YOUR RESPONSE

What are three things that you can do to use this Practical Wisdom in your daily life?

- _____
  _____
  _____
  _____

- _____
  _____
  _____

- _____

"Pride goes before destruction and a haughty spirit before a fall."

Proverbs 16:18 (NKJV)

"This is a verse from the Bible that I am all too familiar with. Foolish pride had been a struggle of mine for years. Being too full of yourself is not attractive to others and causes people to move away, not toward you. The older I get the less I like falling down, because it is a lot harder to get back up."

YOUR REFLECTION

What is the first thing that came to your mind as you read the quote?

_____

_____

_____

_____

YOUR REACTION

Is there a lesson in this quote for you?

_____

_____

_____

_____

YOUR RESPONSE

What are three things that you can do to use this Practical Wisdom in your daily life?

- _____
  _____
  _____
  _____

- _____
  _____
  _____

- _____
  _____

"Unforgiveness is like drinking poison, then waiting for the other person to die."

Anonymous

"There is little doubt that the process of forgiving someone is difficult. The pain associated with the hurt and betrayal is great, but so too is the pain of carrying that hurt with you. Often, as time passes some old wounds begin to heal and restoration of what was broken becomes increasingly more possible."

YOUR REFLECTION

What is the first thing that came to your mind as you read the quote?

_____

_____

_____

_____

_____

YOUR REACTION

Is there a lesson in this quote for you?

_____

_____

_____

_____

_____

YOUR RESPONSE

What are three things that you can do to use this Practical Wisdom in your daily life?

- _____

  _____

  _____

  _____

- _____

  _____

  _____

  _____

- _____

  _____

"The greatest tragedy in life is not death, but life without purpose."

Dr. Myles Munroe Pastor, Teacher, Motivator
1954 - 2014

"This quote is by far one of my favorites because it lets me know that one's purpose in life is what matters most. Everyone is going to die someday, but what will you have left behind? What lives have you touched? What good thing will someone be able to say about you?

YOUR REFLECTION

What is the first thing that came to your mind as you read the quote?

_____

_____

_____

_____

YOUR REACTION

Is there a lesson in this quote for you?

_____

_____

_____

_____

YOUR RESPONSE

What are three things that you can do to use this Practical Wisdom in your daily life?

- _____

  _____

  _____

  _____

- _____

  _____

  _____

- _____

  _____

"We learn wisdom from failure much more than from success."

Samuel Smiles
Scottish Author
and Reformer
1812 – 1904

"The fact that we fail is real and it is okay to acknowledge that it happens. The key regarding failure or failing is what we recognize and understand about how it happened. As we come to this realization, we can make the necessary adjustment as we move forward. We may fail again, but not the same way."

YOUR REFLECTION

What is the first thing that came to your mind as you read the quote?

_____
_____
_____
_____
_____

YOUR REACTION

Is there a lesson in this quote for you?

_____
_____
_____
_____
_____

YOUR RESPONSE

What are three things that you can do to use this Practical Wisdom in your daily life?

- _____

  _____

  _____

- _____

  _____

  _____

- _____

  _____

> *"When I discover who I am, I'll be free."*
>
> *Ralph Ellison Novelist,
> Literary Critic, Scholar
> 1913 - 1994*

"There is nothing more invigorating than self-discovery . . . the process of coming to know oneself better. There was a time when I always saw myself through the eyes of others. This quote says to me that "true freedom" comes when you look into a mirror and are totally pleased with the person looking back at you."

YOUR REFLECTION

What is the first thing that came to your mind as you read the quote?

_____

_____

_____

_____

_____

YOUR REACTION

Is there a lesson in this quote for you?

_____

_____

_____

_____

_____

YOUR RESPONSE

What are three things that you can do to use this Practical Wisdom in your daily life?

- _____

  _____

  _____

  _____

- _____

  _____

  _____

  _____

- _____

  _____

"There is never a right way to do the wrong thing."

*E. Alan Jacobsen
Businessman, Civic Leader
and Friend
1953 - 2019*

"Growing up, I often struggled with doing the right thing. I thank God for changing my heart and helping me to learn a better way to live before it was too late. Today, my integrity and trust mean everything to me. It only takes a moment to lose it all and forfeit the hard work of being a person of true character."

YOUR REFLECTION

What is the first thing that came to your mind as you read the quote?

_____

_____

_____

_____

_____

YOUR REACTION

Is there a lesson in this quote for you?

_____

_____

_____

_____

_____

YOUR RESPONSE

What are three things that you can do to use this Practical Wisdom in your daily life?

- _____
  _____
  _____

- _____
  _____
  _____

- _____
  _____
  _____

"It's not the years in your life, but the life in your years that count."

*Adlai E. Stevenson II
Lawyer, Politician, Diplomat,
2-Time Candidate for President
1900 - 1965*

"We never know about many days that we will get in our lives. We do not control the days, but we can control what we do with those days. I believe that it is critical to see every day as an opportunity to give back to the world. There is no time to waste and no reason not to give everything you have in everything you do."

YOUR REFLECTION

What is the first thing that came to your mind as you read the quote?

_____

_____

_____

_____

_____

YOUR REACTION

Is there a lesson in this quote for you?

_____

_____

_____

_____

_____

YOUR RESPONSE

What are three things that you can do to use this Practical Wisdom in your daily life?

- _____
  _____
  _____
  _____

- _____
  _____
  _____
  _____

- _____
  _____

"Most people don't plan to fail; they just fail to plan."

*John James Beckley
First Librarian of the
U.S. Congress
1757 - 1807*

"I do not believe that anyone wants to intentionally fail. However, if we go through life without any kind of a plan, then we increase our chances of not being successful. I have learned that even having some semblance of a plan is better than just "flying by the seat of your pants." Something is always better than nothing."

YOUR REFLECTION

What is the first thing that came to your mind as you read the quote?

_____

_____

_____

_____

_____

YOUR REACTION

Is there a lesson in this quote for you?

_____

_____

_____

_____

_____

YOUR RESPONSE

What are three things that you can do to use this Practical Wisdom in your daily life?

- _____

  _____

  _____

  _____

- _____

  _____

  _____

- _____

  _____

"Everywhere you can go, isn't somewhere you should go."

Maeola (Harris) Blanchard
My mother and my hero

"When I really think back over my life, I realize that there were places where I should have never been. Fortunately for me, God's hand of protection was with me. The lesson is this . . . as important as it is to know where to be, it is equally as important to know where not to be."

YOUR REFLECTION

What is the first thing that came to your mind as you read the quote?

_____
_____
_____
_____

YOUR REACTION

Is there a lesson in this quote for you?

_____
_____
_____
_____

YOUR RESPONSE

What are three things that you can do to use this Practical Wisdom in your daily life?

- _____
  _____
  _____
  _____

- _____
  _____
  _____

- _____
  _____

> *"The truth that's told with bad intent beats all the lies one can invent."*
>
> **William Blake**
> *English Poet, Painter, Printmaker*
> *1770 - 1845*

"There is never anything wrong with telling the truth. However, when the truth teller has a wrong motive, the truth is tainted and is not told for the well-being of others. What is said though true, will only reveal the darkened heart of the one from whose lips it proceeds."

YOUR REFLECTION

What is the first thing that came to your mind as you read the quote?

_____

_____

_____

_____

_____

YOUR REACTION

Is there a lesson in this quote for you?

_____

_____

_____

_____

_____

YOUR RESPONSE

What are three things that you can do to use this Practical Wisdom in your daily life?

- _____
  _____
  _____
  _____

- _____
  _____
  _____

- _____
  _____

> *"Dreams without goals remain dreams and fuel disappointment."*
>
> **Denzel Washington**
> *Actor, Director, Producer, Community Leader*

"There is nothing wrong or bad about dreaming or envisioning a better future. However, simply dreaming does not make anything happen. You must take concrete steps and real actions toward what you are dreaming about. To do anything less will mean that all of your dreams will amount to nothing."

YOUR REFLECTION

What is the first thing that came to your mind as you read the quote?

_____

_____

_____

_____

YOUR REACTION

Is there a lesson in this quote for you?

_____

_____

_____

_____

YOUR RESPONSE

What are three things that you can do to use this Practical Wisdom in your daily life?

- _____

  _____

  _____

  _____

- _____

  _____

  _____

- _____

  _____

  _____

"The journey of a thousand miles begins with a single step."

Chinese Proverb

"Sometimes the hardest thing to do is to get started. You know what you should do, but you just cannot get moving in the right direction. The key is to begin with the end in mind and take it one step at a time. And know this, nothing will happen, and you will never finish if you do not begin."

YOUR REFLECTION

What is the first thing that came to your mind as you read the quote?

_____

_____

_____

_____

YOUR REACTION

Is there a lesson in this quote for you?

_____

_____

_____

_____

YOUR RESPONSE

What are three things that you can do to use this Practical Wisdom in your daily life?

- _____
  _____
  _____
  _____

- _____
  _____
  _____

- _____
  _____

"Many of life's failures are people who did not realize how close they were to success."

Thomas Alva Edison
Inventor, Innovator
1847 - 1931

"I know that there are times when I might have stopped or quit before I should have. Going for what you want in life takes a great deal of courage, patience and endurance. There are no shortcuts and trying to take them often does not end well. This quote has so much truth in it and calls us to "hang in there."

YOUR REFLECTION

What is the first thing that came to your mind as you read the quote?

_____
_____
_____
_____

_____

YOUR REACTION

Is there a lesson in this quote for you?

_____
_____
_____
_____
_____

YOUR RESPONSE

What are three things that you can do to use this Practical Wisdom in your daily life?

- _____
  _____
  _____
  _____

- _____
  _____
  _____
  _____

- _____
  _____
  _____

"A liar should have a good memory."

*Marcus Fabius Quintilianus
Roman Rhetorician
c. 35 – c. 100 AD*

"Police tell people who get arrested, "You have the right to remain silent. Anything you say can be used against you." They know that the more a person lies, the more that the person thinks that they must continue to lie. It is difficult to tell the exact same story repeatedly if it is a lie. I have found that just telling the truth is the best thing to do."

YOUR REFLECTION

What is the first thing that came to your mind as you read the quote?

_____
_____
_____
_____

_____

YOUR REACTION

Is there a lesson in this quote for you?

_____
_____
_____
_____

YOUR RESPONSE

What are three things that you can do to use this Practical Wisdom in your daily life?

- _____
  _____
  _____
  _____

- _____
  _____
  _____

- _____
  _____

"The dictionary is the only place where success comes before work."

Virgil (Stubby) Currence
Sportswriter, Reporter, Columnist
1904 - 1981

"All too often people are looking for shortcuts and quick fixes instead of making the efforts that make success real. I have learned that somebody is always working on their craft while others are resting. It is not likely that a person will get a maximum return with a minimal investment. It just does not work like that!"

YOUR REFLECTION

What is the first thing that came to your mind as you read the quote?

_____
_____
_____
_____

_____

YOUR REACTION

Is there a lesson in this quote for you?

_____
_____
_____
_____
_____

YOUR RESPONSE

What are three things that you can do to use this Practical Wisdom in your daily life?

- _____

  _____

  _____

  _____

- _____

  _____

  _____

  _____

- _____

  _____

"The time is always right to do what is right."

*Rev. Dr. Martin Luther King, Jr.
Civil Rights Leader
1929 - 1968*

"I have learned over the years that to do what is right requires taking a risk and being open to criticism. Being a champion for justice or an advocate for other is not easy. To be a person who takes a stand or who stands up for others means that you must be a person of character, integrity and fortitude."

YOUR REFLECTION

What is the first thing that came to your mind as you read the quote?

_____
_____
_____
_____

_____

YOUR REACTION

Is there a lesson in this quote for you?

_____
_____
_____
_____
_____

YOUR RESPONSE

What are three things that you can do to use this Practical Wisdom in your daily life?

- _____
  _____
  _____
  _____

- _____
  _____
  _____
  _____

- _____
  _____

"Everything you can do, isn't something you should do."

Maeola (Harris) Blanchard
My mother and my hero

"As a person matures, he or she should develop an ability to discern what is appropriate and what is not. I have learned that just because I like talking to people, does not mean that I need to do so every time I get on an elevator. It is important to use wisdom, understanding the situation before I act."

YOUR REFLECTION

What is the first thing that came to your mind as you read the quote?

_____
_____
_____
_____

YOUR REACTION

Is there a lesson in this quote for you?

_____
_____
_____
_____

YOUR RESPONSE

What are three things that you can do to use this Practical Wisdom in your daily life?

- _____
  _____
  _____
  _____

- _____
  _____
  _____

- _____
  _____

"Humility does not mean not thinking about yourself, but thinking of yourself less often."

E. Alan Jacobsen
Businessman, Civic
Leader and Friend
1953 - 2019

"In an age of "look at me," it is important to keep things in perspective. Humility and vanity do not go together! It is critical that we are "secure in our own skin;" okay with who we are. There is nothing wrong with a little attention, but taken to extremes, it can be quite unbecoming."

YOUR REFLECTION

What is the first thing that came to your mind as you read the quote?

_____

_____

_____

_____

_____

YOUR REACTION

Is there a lesson in this quote for you?

_____

_____

_____

_____

_____

YOUR RESPONSE

What are three things that you can do to use this Practical Wisdom in your daily life?

- _____
  _____
  _____
  _____

- _____
  _____
  _____

- _____
  _____

"You never get a second chance to a make good first impression."

Will Rogers
Humorist, Actor
1879 - 1935

"It is a shame that appearances mean so much in this culture, the superficial over the substantive. It is vital that a person makes a good impression, however, there are likely no "do-overs." I have found that it is critical that I do my best to make sure that "I am memorable," for all the right reasons."

YOUR REFLECTION

What is the first thing that came to your mind as you read the quote?

_____
_____
_____
_____
_____

YOUR REACTION

Is there a lesson in this quote for you?

_____
_____
_____
_____
_____

YOUR RESPONSE

What are three things that you can do to use this Practical Wisdom in your daily life?

- _____

  _____

  _____

  _____

- _____

  _____

  _____

- _____

  _____

"You don't have to be great to start, but you have to start to be great!"

*Hilary Hinton "Zig" Ziglar
American Author, Salesman
and Motivational Speaker
1926 - 2012*

"Thinking back, I can remember so many people who saw in me something that I could not see in myself. Some people even told me that I had true greatness in me. When I finally realized that greatness is not a destination, but a journey . . . I began to move in its direction and have never looked back."

YOUR REFLECTION

What is the first thing that came to your mind as you read the quote?

_____
_____
_____
_____
_____

YOUR REACTION

Is there a lesson in this quote for you?

_____
_____
_____
_____
_____

YOUR RESPONSE

What are three things that you can do to use this Practical Wisdom in your daily life?

- _____
  _____
  _____

- _____
  _____
  _____

- _____
  _____
  _____

"Practical Wisdom" from John

Over the years, I have said some quotes that could be considered simple, but profound. I want to share these twenty-five (25) of my favorite and often used quotes with you. I believe that you will find among these quotes, **"practical wisdom"** that will impact you and make a difference in your life.

1.) "What is life if not a gift and what good is a gift unless you give it away?"

2.) "You don't have anything if you don't have hope."

3.) "Don't treat others the way you want to be treated . . . treat them better."

4.) "It's not that you have fallen down that matters, but what you have learned when you get back up."

5.) "Don't just value and appreciate people for what they do, but do so for who they are."

After reading John's quotes, is there one that stands out to you? Write down your thoughts and what the quote(s) mean to you.

6.) "You don't have to be the boss to be a leader."

7.) "It's not always the big things a person does that has the greatest impact."

8.) "Sometimes you just have to find a way."

9.) "Excellence is the only option."

10.) "If you don't know where you are going, it doesn't matter what road you take."

11.) "Who are you encouraging?"

12.) "Life is much too short to live it with grudges and regrets."

13.) "I don't have time for foolishness."

14.) "Complaining is not a strategy."

15.) "Everybody wants to go to Heaven, but nobody wants to die."

16.) "Gratitude is the one of the few things that offers maximum return on a minimal investment."

After reading John's quotes, is there one that stands out to you? Write down your thoughts and what the quote(s) mean to you.

17.) "There is rarely a good reason for being late to something important."

18.) "There is no us and them, there is just us."

19.) "When you mess up, 'fess up."

20.) "Encourage someone today!"

21.) "If you could have changed it yourself, you would have by now."

22.) "You can choose your choices, but you cannot always choose the consequences."

23.) "We are all a work in progress."

24.) "Where there is a problem, there is always a solution."

25.) "I know what's wrong with everyone else, but what do I see when I look in the mirror"?

After reading John's quotes, is there one that stands out to you? Write down your thoughts and what the quote(s) mean to you.

*"As I have thought about this book, I realize that just about everyone has said or heard something that could considered "practical wisdom." Think about the people in your life and the things they have said. Use the next few pages as your own journal of quotes, phrases and sayings. Don't forget to **REFLECT, REACT** AND **RESPOND** to what you have written."*

WRITE YOUR OWN "PRACTICAL WISDOM"

Encouragement Unlimited, Inc. is a tax-exempt charitable organization. To know more about the organization and its mission, check out its website: www.encouragementunlimited.org.

To support the organization, tax deductible donations can be sent to:
**Encouragement Unlimited, Inc.
P. O. Box 84734
Lincoln, NE 68501**

Scan this QR code to directly to the Encouragement Unlimited website

ABOUT THE AUTHOR

John Leonard Harris aka "Mr. Encouragement" is a native of St. Louis (Wellston), Missouri. He is the Founder and President of Encouragement Unlimited, Inc., a charitable nonprofit organization that he founded in 2002 to serve people from all walks of life. He has been a speaker, educator, and motivator for over 20 years.

Mr. Harris earned a bachelor's degree in Radio-TV-Film Production from the University of Missouri-Columbia and his master's degree in Education from the University of Nebraska-Lincoln.

Mr. Harris has worked as a Senior Pastor, corporate trainer, and military employment coach. He is an actor, author, and sports broadcaster. **He is a published author, winning the "Article of the Year" award for his article, "The Portrayal of the Black Family in Primetime Network Television."** He also wrote, "The Search for Self: Examining Black Racial Identity and Intergroup Conflict" which was published in the Journal of Intergroup Relations in 2000. He served as a Community Columnist for the Lincoln Journal Star and has been a contributing writer for "For Husker Fans Only."

Likely his greatest achievement is his marriage to his wife, Charlene of nearly 35 years and the raising of their four children, Preston, Shannon, JoAnna and John Jr. He and Charlene have three grandsons, Eli, Legend and Owen.

To know more about John Leonard Harris, just **GOOGLE** his name or visit the Encouragement Unlimited website.